Look at Me

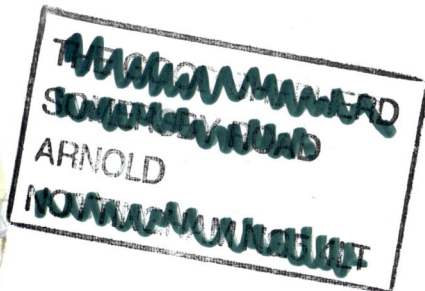

by **Anne Giulieri**

illustrated by **Susy Boyer**

Here is my brush.

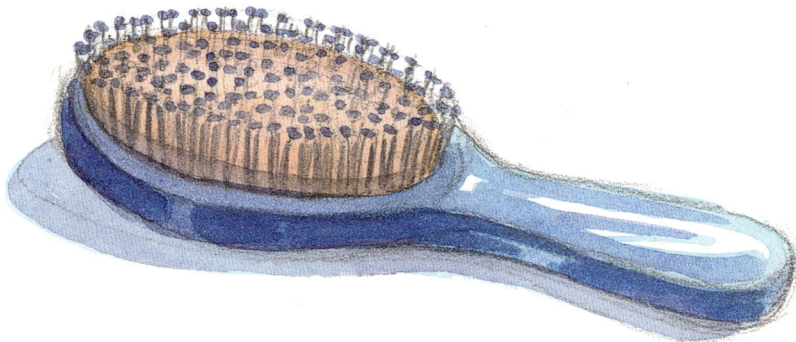

Look at me.

Here is my breakfast.

Look at me.

Here is my lunch.

Look at me.

Here is my bag.

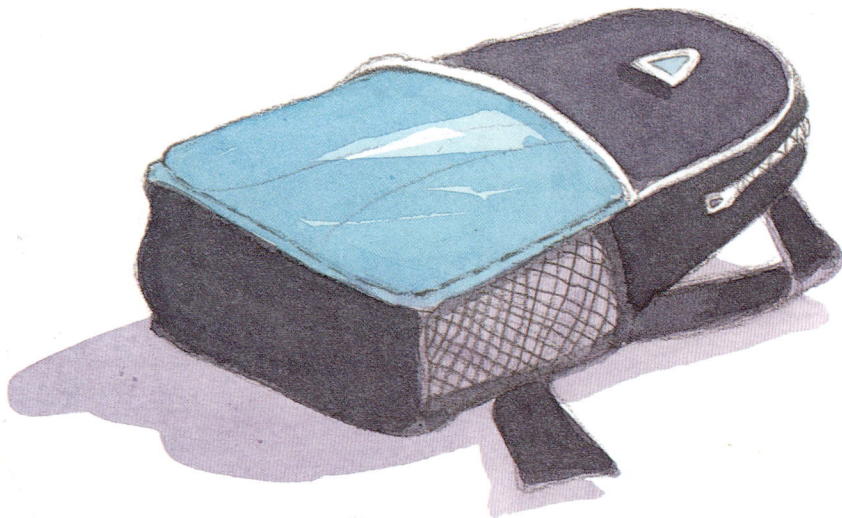

Look at me.

Here is my bike.

Look at me.

Here is my friend.

Look at me.

13

Here is my book.

Look at me.

Here is my teacher.
Look at me.